AF508567

Finding God at a Garage Sale
Love, Miracles & Old Shoes

Lessons learned from junk

...Follow the signs...

Copyright 2021 - Monica Today

Dedication

This book is dedicated to my grandpa, Charles "Chuck" Wollborg, who passed away just three months before the completion of this book. I feel his presence with me as I write this and know that he is watching over me with love and pride for a job well done.

Grandpa taught us through his actions that hard work, education, persistence and follow-through were the keys to excellence and that each of us contain that excellence within us. He taught us that if you love something, you take care of it. If you love someone, you take care of them and that includes taking care of oneself.

My grandpa would spend hours teaching us how to water ski, how to drive or how to tie a knot just right. A job wasn't complete until is was done correctly. A job well-done was well rewarded, however, and our family cabin had plaques all over the walls with handmade "awards" printed and framed with each of his grandchildren's names and accomplishments written upon them.

I'll never forget when I learned that Grandpa had brushed the dog's teeth every night before bed! I laugh to myself as i think of it now.

To my grandma, Virginia "Toody" Wollborg, who shared that same spirit of excellence. Her strength and determination was the backbone of a multimillion dollar company, founded by a woman, in a time when female entrepreneurs were much less common. Her favorite saying, "The harder you work, the luckier you get." Her drive was complemented by true empathy and tenderness. Sharing your journey with my grandmother meant being supported by compassionate ears and often compassionate tears. Through my grandparents' actions, I learned about the importance of graciousness, respect and generosity.

To my mother, Cindi Valverde, who taught me to express my unique soul in this lifetime and to celebrate and honor the expressions of others as the priceless gifts that they are. It is through honoring others' perspectives that I am able to connect with them and with myself on a deep and meaningful level.

It is because of my mother's appreciation of art and music that I have felt empowered as a visual artist, a singer and a writer of music and poetry. My mother and my stepdad, Steve Valverde have shown me that artists can live a life that is both grounded and inspirational at the same time.

To my son, Saint, who has challenged me more than any person in my life. Everything that I claim to be or espouse, he holds a mirror up to, prompting me to live my truth rather than to simply speak my ideals. Saint is strong, intelligent and independent, leaving me to find my approval of self from within rather than seeking it from others.

To my sister, Lisa, who simply "gets me" in ways that I do not have the words to express, although she always does. Lisa's consistent kindness through times of immense struggle boggles my mind.
To my brother, Matt, who prioritizes being a good person. Matt is an inspiration to our entire family, teaching us to not waste time on circumstances that drain or defeat us but to keep our eyes on the goal.

To my other-in-law, Claudia, who is kind, humble and consistently supportive, even when my "Five-year plan" may turn out be a "Forty-year reality."

To my Songbird, partner and best friend, Matthew Schriver. When we met, our wings were broken; today we fly and sing together. You are patient, kind, attentive and the best kisser in the universe. You roll with every hair-brained scheme that I concoct and I am truly grateful for your love.

To my friends, family and clients, both in body and in Heaven. Thank you for listening to me, for letting me share messages from your loved ones with you. Thank you for loving me, for laughing with me, for crying with me.

Thank you for embracing my weirdo, sometimes potty-mouthed behavior, my periods of introverted withdrawal, my hypochondriacal rants, my spontaneous outbursts, my strange fear of "driving south"and my obsession with starting a "pudding bar" (but seriously, who wouldn't love a pudding bar?)

It is because of your open hearts and willingness to listen, even when it hurt, that we have been able to deeply connect. I cherish each and every one of you.

Prologue

I used to shop at garage sales for bargains...now I stop at garage sales for wisdom. I am in awe of the love that I have found at garage sales. Let me paint the picture of a recent encounter I experienced through the eyes of extreme gratitude.

Act 1, scene 1: I wander about town and everywhere I go I see colorful signs created with care by strangers inviting me on a tour of their driveway or garage. The signs excite my curiosity and inform me that this curiosity will be fulfilled near instantaneously...only 4 feet ahead!

I arrive at the destination and excitedly open the car door in eager anticipation of what's to come. I walk slowly toward the house...I actually want to run, but I resist the temptation. Seconds later a furry little creature comes running to welcome me (he didn't resist the temptation to run!)

I bend down with a smile as he excitedly licks my toes through my sandals. We approach the sale, now together, my new furry friend and I, his head held high, a job well-done.

As I reach the edge of the driveway, I am now greeted by a child selling treats, standing tall with pride as great as any seasoned CEO.
I happily feast on a cookie and sip from a cup of juice that likely they were charging less for than the paper cup that it was poured into. The juice is so sour that the back corners of my mouth start to salivate and my smile grows as I imagine the valiant effort required to make this juice.

I thank the little girl and express to her how impressed I am with her stand...she rises an inch or so taller.
As I travel further into the sale, I greet the eyes of two smiling friends

sunbathing in now .50-cent lawn chairs. I express to them the joy that I have encountered so far and thank them for being there.

One woman rises from her chair and lovingly shares with me the stories that these treasures carry. "This belonged to my mother, she loved to crochet, she would sit in that chair over there and crochet for hours on end. It was made to cover the toilet paper roll on the back of the toilet" she looks toward the ground a bit embarrassed "Kind of silly" she says.

I say, "I think it's wonderful how much care people take in making things special" she lifted her head up and smiled.

"Yes, she used to always do stuff like that."
She gestured toward the rest of the table laden with kitty cat potholders and teapot cozies. "She passed last year and I am

just now getting around to going through her things." I smile and tell her that we all process things in our own time and she smiles back.

 I think to myself how grateful I am to have been guided here to this garage sale and that this sweet woman was afforded the opportunity to visit with her mother as we spoke of her.

We continue to go over the stories of other items at the sale, the three of us ladies laughing over items that had been held onto for years and speculating as to the purpose of others. So much time had passed that another drink and cookie were in order and our diligent stand owner was at the ready.

It was now time to go and we happily exchanged information vowing to stay in touch. I packed my bag full of potholders, toilet paper holders and spare cookies into the car and waved goodbye.

I've learned a lot about myself at garage sales. I've learned about perception and that the way that I experience my day...my life ...comes down to a single moment's interaction. People invite us into their homes, into their hearts every day. They give us the opportunity to hear them, to understand them and even to heal them.

 When we take these opportunities, these are the ways in which we are healed as well.

Processing and grieving is not simply something that happens at funerals or wakes. We are constantly processing and sharing our burdens and joys with all of those that we come into contact with. My grandmother used to crochet potholders just like that and my uncle used those exact pens for his drawings.

I've become a better artist by going to garage sales. I've learned about how things were made and the resourceful things that people can do with a bottle

cap and a shoe horn...I've learned what a
shoe horn is!

I've learned that many people will spend
hours in the hot sun working for change
or buying a superfluous amount of
potholders for the opportunity to have an
inspiring and healing conversation.
I've learned that the remnants of past
lives and memories that I have collected
over the years make up who I am as a
person.

I am a product of all of the bits and
pieces of history that came before me...a
compilation from the the Garage Sale of
the Universe...where nothing is
discarded, only laid out onto white sheets
to be recombined in any infinite number
of ways.

I was not merely born, I was recycled…
repurposed from bits of leftover stardust
and shimmering butterfly wings...from
golden threads of wheat and sparkling

silver sand stirred together with intention and destined to rise up and
serve those that come to feast on my inspiration.
It is not possible for me to be
"unwanted," "unattractive,"
"undesirable" or any of those other "un"
words one might hear.

My body has developed a very unique filtration system. "Un" might meet my ears, but reaches my soul as "in"
I hear "invincible," I hear "insightful," I hear "inspirational."
It is my choice how I see the world...whether or not I view an interaction as trivial or sacred, whether or not i choose a moment to fill me with resentment or gratitude or whether I make the choice to see my life experience as Trash or as Treasure.

My name is Monica a.k.a. The Garbage Collector. When I was little, I was caught pulling a glass aspirin bottle out of the trash and earned that nickname. I had been rescuing the bottle to use as a vase to put tiny flowers in. The name even had a jingle to go with it:

Monica is a garbage collector, a garbage collector she is!

The name and song were meant to be shaming, but fortunately, I don't shame easily and went on to not only embrace my habit of seeing beauty in trash but to make a living out of it.

Over the years I have come to find not only beauty in trash but profound wisdom as well. Objects tell stories, serve as symbols, signs and gateways to infinite pathways of understanding.

I have learned that perceived mistakes are merely an opportunity for new perspectives. By seeing the world in this manner I have also come to see that when we embrace life's realities, when our eyes, hearts and minds are open, that is when we are able to experience miracles.

Table of Contents

73. The Free Box
Release what no longer serves you

The Glue
Be resourceful

As a child I received a bottle of glue one Christmas. I had been absolutely thrilled! To me glue wasn't just glue, it was toy dolls, toadstools and fairy crowns. Today, as a professional Trash Artist, my trash fashions have won awards, walked runways in Los Angeles and Seattle, have appeared on television and are currently offered for sale in museums, stores and galleries. That .25-cent bottle of glue was the best investment my mom ever made.

If you find yourself stuck, wanting to be someone or somewhere else, wishing you were happier for whatever reason, stop and take a look around. Ask yourself what you have to work with and start combining it in different ways to solve a problem or to come up with a fun new concept.

With a resourceful mindset, you'll never
stay stuck for long!

24

The Sculpture
Consider different perspectives

One of the artists that lived in our town was a sculptor named Dennis Patton. Dennis lived right on our block, about ten houses away from ours.

It was clear that Dennis was an artist because in our neighborhood of humble walkways and plain cement drives, Dennis had a front yard of dry grass and a larger than life metal lady sprawled out across it. Dennis had been the creator of some very iconic sculptures in Marin County.

He was a fascinating man and one that I aspired to emulate in some form in my life, so when we were asked to do a report in school on someone that was an inspiration to us, I seized the opportunity to do an interview with him. To this day, this was the strangest and most impactful interview of any artist that I've interviewed.

 I was a freshman in high school and remember walking down the street to his house with just a pad of paper and a pencil, feeling thoroughly intimidated. Even though I had been just a high school student, I had been beating myself up the whole way down there. *Who was I to interview this famous artist? What do I know about art? What will I even ask him?*

When I arrived, Dennis greeted me graciously and walked me through the house where he had his art displayed throughout. When we got back to the front driveway, he pointed to a jumble of wire that was several feet tall.

"And here's my masterpiece," he said.

I started to shake and fumble over my words, trying to make sense of what was in front of me. After letting me squirm for a short while, he said,

 "No, I'm just messin' with ya'."

I laughed nervously.

"Okay, now come over here," he said as he led me to a long wire that stuck straight out of the middle of the sculpture.

 The wire had a hoop at the end of it, which he instructed me to stoop down and look through. Through that crudely bent, oval loophole was an image of Einstein, the details making the depiction near photographic. The kink to his eyebrows, the glimmer in his eyes, the furrow in his brow, astounding! I had stood here just seconds before, no awareness of what was before me. Trying to see Einstein at any other angle would have been futile. There were no walls, there was no door, no discernible entry way in, yet this loophole was in fact a keyhole without even the need for a key.

This experience has served me in my life in so many ways. When I believe that someone should get me or see things from where I stand, I am reminded that people are only able to comprehend things from their place and time in the moment. When I stand in my truth and live a life that is inspirational to me, people will be more likely to want to come over and learn more about my perspective.

The Bread Bag Tabs
Release attachment to outcomes

My mom's dad was the inventor of those little tabs that you see on bread bags. He actually created them for the Apple industry in Wenatchee, Washington. He didn't get the patent on them however - the patent went to the man who created the machines to produce them. I had always resented that my he hadn't gotten the credit for that. I had watched both my mom and myself work hard only to have people steal our ideas once the work had been done. One day I'd asked my mom if she had been resentful as well, considering all the sacrifice of time and effort he had made. I had made a point to remind her of how poor she had been as a child.

My mom said something that shook me awake: "No," she said. M dad was an artist, he just loved the process of coming up with ideas."

Years later, my mom would go on to invent an idea of her own called the washable produce bag. My mom had been tired of using disposable plastic bags for her produce and decided to use some yellow tulle netting left over from a project to sew some bags to re-use. The bags ended up taking off. Years later, at a trade show in Florida, it just so happened that the manufacturer of the bread tab was only booths down from my mom. She went up to the man at the booth and said, "My dad was the one that invented that tab."

The man said, "Actually, my grandfather invented the tab. He thought of the idea

while returning from a business trip to
Wenatchee, Washington"

 My mom replied, "We're from
Wenatchee, Washington."

But that synchronistic encounter wasn't
about settling a grudge. It was the
universe's way of winking at my mom
and acknowledging what she had
accomplished. She had taken what she
had learned from her father and made it
her own. She had taken it to a level
beyond not only creation but to follow-
through. I write this with tears in my eyes
as I realize that writing about this story
is my way of making it my own.

What I've come to understand is that
what I think, what my judgment or
opinion is about how a situation should
or shouldn't have happened, often comes
up short. The ego can only factor in the

limited data of what it has experienced or what it has been told by others. My happiness comes from observing how life is unfolding and through the recognition of how it's serving me.

The Pink Scarf
Music heals

In my early 20s we went to see my ex-husband's cousin who was an Elvis Presley impersonator. His name was Bruno, he was only 10 years old and they had called him "Little Elvis."
We had flown to Hawaii from California and before we left, Jimmie's grandmother had told us that her half brother Eugene (Bruno's grandfather) had survived execution in the Philippines many years ago. She said that the soldiers had been chopping off heads and that the only reason that he had survived was because they had gotten tired and only partially cut through his neck. He had been able to play dead, then hold his head up and walk himself to get help.

During the performance Bruno passed out pink scarves to the audience and I received one. I still have the photo of me with my pink scarf. After the performance I looked at the back of Eugene's neck and there was the scar.

Many years later we got word of Bruno's huge success. Many of you know him today as "Bruno Mars." Bruno's grandfather had needed to live so that generations later, Bruno could be born and bring music into our world.

Never underestimate the power of music to heal across matter, space and time.

The Computer
Everything is connected

In my early 20s my dad died. After his passing, my sister, my brother and I had gone to the house where he had lived. Holding one another's hands in a circle had given us the strength to walk through the house together. My dad had loved technology and had left behind his computer.

Eventually I would end up with my father's computer, although my sister had been the one that had communicated with him on it the most. My brother-in-law at the time had experience with computers and had tried all day to get around a lock that had been placed on it. After hours of effort and replacement of a melted cable, Mike had gotten through.

On the black screen, in green lettering appeared this message:

Pollyanna, Goodbye and good luck, love Dad, (Mav)

I was "Pollyanna" and my dad was "Maverick" (from the movie Top Gun.)

At the time, I had gone over and over the reasons that I had been the one to receive the message, a message written directly to me.

Years later, on the morning of my 35th birthday, I would share that story with friends. Later that same afternoon i had been reflecting upon the experience while driving home from an art show. I turned on the radio and a man spoke these exact words "We're talking about communicating with the afterlife through technology." I had chills.

Modern computers have shown us that we are all connected, able to reach one another across the world through one universal language, a translation of dots and dashes.

Although we may not understand the hows, there are infinite ways that we are connected to everyone and everything. Even the death of the body will not keep us apart. When loved ones pass, we just learn new ways of communicating with them.

Family Photos
Don't let your past define you

Three months ago my grandfather passed, leaving behind a box of slides and VHS cassettes. On the videos I saw the pain behind my eyes and began reliving trauma from my earlier life. After diving deeply into the past, I soon was able to return to clarity in the present moment.

As traumatic as the experiences of my childhood had been, those experiences were what had strengthened and shaped me into the person that I am today. When someone shares with me the trauma of sexual abuse, suicide or loss, it is my experiences that allow me to comfort them with true compassion and understanding.

Embrace your past as it is what your wisdom is built upon.

The Birdcage
Release yourself from victimhood

In my late 30s, I had become bitter due to abuse and hardships that I had experienced. I remember my brother having come for a visit and saying, "Moni, you seem a lot more negative now than you used to be."

As painful as that had been to hear, I knew that he had been right. I had been feeling trapped in my relationship, waiting for changes that just never seemed to happen. I had decided to go to a support group for co-dependents. At the group was a woman who had said to me "We sure are addicted to our addicts, aren't we?"

I paused, ready to defend myself. *I'm not an addict*, I thought.

Years of desperation flashed before my eyes. Today, I've come to realize that addiction is a behavior sorely lacking in creativity. Addiction is based upon a belief that it is only one source that is capable of fulfilling one's needs. I had been going to that same source, again and again, looking for answers. She was correct, I was an addict.

I quickly re-evaluated my response and replied.

"Yeah, that's so true."

When I stopped looking for peace outside of myself, I was able to start giving to myself what I had been asking for from others, I had unlocked my freedom.

The Lemonade Stand
Find joy in the successes of others

A couple weekends ago, I pulled over to
a garage sale with a lemonade stand. I
always stop at lemonade stands, period.
While I waited for my lemonade, a boy
with
Down syndrome got off the bus. I learned
that his name was Thomas. He had come
up to me excitedly, showing me his new
doll. He proceeded to tell me what the
attributes were of a "good doll" versus a
"bad doll." I quickly learned that to
Thomas, the "crusty" dolls were no good.

I told Thomas that I go to a lot of garage
sales and that I was going to be on the
lookout for just the doll that he was after.
Thomas got really excited and clapped
his hands and I knew that I had my work
cut out for me.

I told Thomas that when I got the doll, I
would put it in his mailbox.

Last week I was having a challenging evening, having accidentally watched an especially disturbing scene in a movie. As I tried to shift my perspective, the thought of Thomas and his mission made me smile.

Yesterday I found just the doll that Thomas had wanted at a garage sale. A very kind woman had given it to me from her own basket once I had told her the story. Last night we stuffed it in Thomas' mailbox. It made me smile all over again thinking about how excited he would be.

When you learn to find happiness in the joy of others, you give to yourself the gift of a well of joy that never runs dry.

The Money Box
Know your worth

I've seen vastly different pricing at garage sales. At one place and item might sell for a quarter, while at another place it might sell for $10. There are a couple different things that tend to influence an item's value. The first factor is how badly the person wants to get rid of it. If a person doesn't appreciate it, they are more likely to undervalue an item. If a person tells a really good story about an item, full of intriguing mystery or sentiment, the item likely has a higher price tag. Sometimes a buyer will come along and try to point out flaws in an item, trying to negotiate a lower price.

What many people don't realize, however,
is that garage sales and stores aren't the only places that set prices.

We put a value on our worth every single
day with the thoughts that we think and
the choices that we make.
At birth, each of us are inherently
valuable. Someone might come into your
life and recognize the shiny sparkly parts
within you, while someone else might
come along and place you in the free
pile.

We determine our value by the stories
that we choose to believe about
ourselves. When we recognize our
inherent value we will not stop until we
find the people that mirror back to us that
same value.
When you recognize your own worth,
you teach others what your value is.

The Books
Be a student of life

In this lifetime, as accomplished as one person might be, no one person can know everything. There exists what I call the "Me" mind and the "We" mind.

The "Me" mind is focused on the protection of the body, making judgments and decisions based upon the limitations of their personal experience or brain capacity.

The "We" mind reaches out to the vastness of space time and understanding, factoring in the experiences of all. At garage sales, I am always led to exactly the right wisdom that I am ready to receive.

To be a student of life is to be a listener and to embrace insight in whatever form that it is given.

The Shoes
Trust the journey

In my mid-40s, I started to see synchronicities everywhere that I went. I had been doing lots of self-improvement work. I had created a website inspired by a speech by Wayne Dyer that had talked about a tribe that had gathered together to build up troubled members of their society. The site was called "Speaking of you" and it served as a virtual space to show gratitude for others.

Not long after creating the site, I got a call from a girlfriend of mine asking me if I wanted to sell CDs for her singer friend Tari. Tari would be the opening act for a guy out in Glendale. I asked her who the guy was and she replied, "His name is Wayne Dyer"

I headed out the morning of the event and my car broke down. I called a tow truck and had it towed home. Once home, I rented a car. My ex-husband had been furious, but I knew that I had to be there. I finally got to the event and opened the doors, a strong woosh of air-conditioning blew onto me and the song amazing grace was playing over the speakers. Tears welled up in my eyes.

At that event I had gained knowledge that has served me immensely in my life. Had I not trusted that voice, had i listened to my fear or limitation, I could've easily talked myself out of going.

Trusting the journey means putting one foot in front of the other, knowing that wherever you end up, you will receive the wisdom that you are meant to receive.

The Peanut Grinder
Find the humor

I raised my daughter in the hills of Malibu California. I was an artist we lived in tiny spaces and I took on as many odd jobs as was necessary to pay the rent. One of the jobs that I worked at was in the produce department. I worked with a guy named Bob who was a very matter-of-fact guy, I believe Bob had been Autistic.

My job had been to keep the customers happy. If there was any issue with customers, I would be the one to resolve it.

In Malibu, we had both a peanut machine and an almond machine at the edge of the Produce Department. The machines were always having issues, but the store had kept them available due to the high demand from Malibu locals for fresh nut butters.

One day Bob had come up to me, more upset than usual. Rolling his eyes in annoyance, he said,

"MacGyver over there with the peanut machine."

I had wondered what kind of trouble I was in for as I headed over to the machines. As I got closer, I saw a familiar yet unexpected face.

There standing in front of me was Richard Dean Anderson. The actual actor that played MacGyver in the show.
I laughed to myself, Bob's reaction replaying in my mind.

If you look up the word MacGyver in the dictionary it is actually a verb, meaning:

"To make or repair something in an improvised or inventive way, making use of whatever items are at hand."

The Seashells
Appreciate the little things

This lesson is a short and sweet reminder of the joy in the simple things like walking on the beach, lighting a candle and dancing in the rain. Sometimes the most obvious sources of joy are the ones that are overlooked. Take a break, go pick a flower and put it in a pretty little vase.

The Keys
The right doors will open

Two months ago I had woken up to a post online of an estate sale. The sale was nearly 20 minutes south of us, but I just had to be there.

Once at the sale I had learned that the reason they were having the sale was that the owner of the home had recently passed. Her daughter, who was running the sale, had told me that her mother had been in her 90s, that her husband had passed already and that they had been married for 70 years!

As I walked through the house, I felt the love. I took some photos of things that inspired me or made me laugh.

I had taken a photo of a four leaf clover cross stitch on the mantle of the fireplace with a sweet Irish saying.

As we went over the items, Easter decor for my yard, a portable shampoo bowl for my 95-year-old grandpa, items from her parents' world travels - the woman thanked me for my appreciation of them.

 "It has been my experience that only the body dies, that their spirit lives on," I told her.

"Thank you so much," she replied.

Three weeks later, I got a message from my sister saying that they were going to an open house and asking me if I wanted to meet them there later. I told her that I had an appointment but that I could drive down to take a look outside.

As I neared the location, I recognized the lighthouse on the right, as lighthouses always remind me that my husband Matt's Auntie Carol is watching over us.

As fate would have it, the home that my sister had been looking at was the exact house that I had been at the prior month.

My sister shared with me that the last place that they had looked had lots of offers and that someone had made a high cash offer and that had ended the sale. They had been concerned that the same thing was going to happen in this seller's market.

I told the two of them that if they wanted this house, they were going to have to appeal to the mom on the other side, to ask for her help.

I talked to my mom and she said that she had a feeling about this house. The other one just hadn't felt right, but this one did.

My mom is a Buddhist, and said that she would chant for it. We both agreed that it just had to happen because I needed to write about it in my book Finding God at a garage sale.

 I sent a message to Lisa of a song that came up that I knew was meant for them - Bonnie Raitt's "Feels Like Home" as listening to it brought me to tears of gratitude.

My sister then told me that they were putting in an offer. Theirs was number 11 of 11 offers.

We soon heard the news, out of those 11 offers, theirs had been accepted.

The day that they moved in, family gathered to celebrate and to help them unpack. A song came on the radio "I will be your lucky penny, you can be my four-leaf clover... starting over." #ChrisStapleton

Outside, a double rainbow shined over them and their new house; it was such a blessing and sign from above. We all took photos in amazement. Just after Easter, my grandpa passed. I am certain that this rainbow was him smiling down on all of us from Heaven.

The Dog
Let yourself be loved

Several years ago I had been at a garage sale when some little kids walked by the with a small dog.

I commented "What a cute little dog you have."

"He's not ours; we don't know whose he is," one of the boys replied.

I had ended up volunteering to take the dog home with me and had left my phone number with the woman that was having the sale. That night my husband and I both fell absolutely in love with her. The next day we got a call from the owner who had been searching for her. She said that she had gotten out frequently and I told her that if she ever needed a home for her to please let me know.

About six months later, the young woman said that she would be having to leave the state and asked if we would keep her. I said that we would.

We had our little girl, "Teenie tiny" for five years until her passing at 13. We had realized that it was finally time to get a dog again when we had watched a movie called "Red Dog."

Right after the movie, I had gotten into the car and driven up the street. I couldn't believe it because in the car was playing a song called "Red Dog." I had pulled over to record the song for Matt.

Teeny tiny had been a black and white dog and so we knew that she had been directing us to our next dog. As I got in the car and I looked up at the sky, there was a rainbow over the area where we had buried Teenie Tiny.

As I write this story, I am sitting here next to our little dog named Sweet Pea. We rescued Sweet Pea from a local shelter. She is our little strawberry blonde angel.

The Decorations
Celebrate change

Holiday decorations are a wonderful reminder that the seasons always bring newness. As I write this, we are going through a heat wave and strawberry season is nearing its end. There are benefits to every season. Sometimes when things change, our first response is to mourn the loss. It can be so comforting, however, to remind ourselves that this change brings fresh experiences and opportunity for joy, connection and friendship.

The Angels 11:11
Have faith

One afternoon I had gone to a friend's hockey game. Before the game I had been having a conversation with another friend about seeing the numbers 11:11.

She had said that it meant that the angels are watching over you. At the game, I had been sitting high up in the bleachers by myself and a little girl, around four 4 years old, headed directly toward me. The little girl stood right in front of me with a notepad in her hand like a junior reporter. She asked me what my name was and told me that hers was Maggie.

Maggie drew a little squiggle of a face on her notepad and without any further conversation, looked me straight in the eyes and asked me "Did you see American Idol last night?"

"No," I replied. "I didn't. Was it good?"

"Oh you should see it, it was on channel Eleven. Eleven, Eleven, Eleven, Eleven." She repeated out loud as she wrote the numbers down on her notepad.

I looked down at the piece of paper with all of the 11s on it in shock as she tore it out of her notebook and handed it to me with care.

That night, I looked up what the last American Idol had been about. They had had a gospel choir on the show, everyone had been wearing long white robes. This had been the only time that this had ever been done before.

The Ring
Be of service

At one garage sale, I had purchased a cluster of jewelry all jumbled together. Having a passion for jewelry, I have a keen eye for pieces that are valuable.

Embedded within the jumble, I had spotted a sterling silver ring with a blue stone. When the woman gave me a price, it was for the entire jumble. I had not pointed out that there had been a sterling silver ring within the jumble. After the sale, every time I would go to wear the ring, I would feel pangs of shame,

feeling that I had been sneaky by not bringing the ring to her attention.
I decided to ask myself where it was that I had felt so desperate that I had gone against what made me feel good about myself.